Sports Stars

WILLIAM PERRY

The Refrigerator

By Andre Roberts

CHILDRENS PRESS®
CHICAGO

Cover photograph: Nawrocki Stock Photo, © Carl V. Sissac
Inside photographs courtesy of the following:
Journalism Services, © Rick Maiman, pages 6, 8, 10, and 25
AP/Wide World Photographs, pages 11, 13, 15, 16, 18, 21, 28, 29, 31, 33, 34, 36, 38, 40, and 42
Nawrocki Stock Photo, © Carl V. Sissac, pages 22, 23, and 29
© Bill Smith, page 39

Author's Dedication to E. R.

In learning to understand the certainties of this brief existence, its realities become less frightening. All too soon, death becomes an accepted member of the family, and life's most important occupation becomes survival. The gifts left to enjoy must be encountered and administered. This then, is the gift of life!

The author would like to give special thanks to William Perry and David Kaiser of Bry and Associates.

Library of Congress Cataloging-in-Publication Data

Roberts, Andre.
    William Perry, the Refrigerator.

    (Sports stars)
    Summary: A brief biography of the 358-pound lineman of the Chicago Bears football team.
    1. Perry, William, 1962-   —Juvenile literature.
2. Football players—United States—Biography—Juvenile literature.   3.   Chicago Bears (Football team)—Juvenile literature.   [1. Perry, William, 1962-   .   2. Football players.   3. Afro-Americans—Biography]   I. Title.
II. Series.
GV939.P47R63   1986   796.332'092'4 [B] [92]   86-4184
ISBN 0-516-04358-7

Sports Stars

WILLIAM PERRY

The Refrigerator

A 358-pound lineman? Who would pick him? What football team would want him? The Chicago Bears. That's who.

Football season is fun. Football fans love the sport. They watch the games. They watch the playoffs. They watch the Super Bowl. Then it's over.

At the beginning of the 1985 season, not many fans knew who William Perry was.

But not really. Not for the real fans. There is still the draft. In the spring, the National Football League teams go to the draft. They pick college players. The teams take turns. They pick the best players. The best player is Number 1.

In April of 1985 the Chicago Bears took their first pick. They picked William Perry. He wasn't considered the best. He was number 22. But the Bears picked him.

Fans were surprised. Why pick a 358-pound lineman? And who picked him? Mike Ditka, the head coach, picked him.

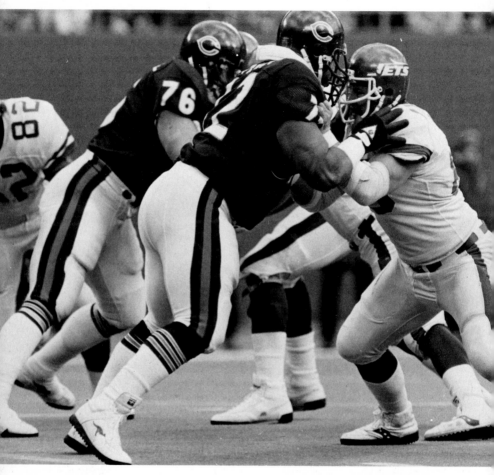

Above: One reason William was picked is because he is a good blocker.
Right: At the Bears' camp, William worked out with his teammates.

William was big when he played in college. He weighed a lot. He was 6 feet 2 inches tall. Another team would need two men to block him. He was strong. He could block well. He could sack the quarterback. But, best of all, he was fast. He ran the 40-yard dash in 5.36 seconds.

But the Bear fans weren't happy. The press wasn't happy. Buddy Ryan, the man who coached the Bears' defense, wasn't happy.

William went to summer training camp. He was weighed. Another Bear player said William was a biscuit away from 350 pounds. The players called him "biscuit."

Hollie and Inez Perry, William's parents

The Bears practiced. The fans still wondered. Who was William Perry? Why was William picked?

William was born on December 16, 1962 in Aiken, South Carolina, to Hollie and Inez Perry. He weighed 13½ pounds at birth. He is the tenth child in a family of twelve children. There are eight boys and four girls.

The Perry brothers liked sports. They played at school. Outside of school they made their own team. They played neighborhood kids. They almost always won. All the brothers are big.

After the Refrigerator became well known, he did commercials. He advertised long underwear and posed with a 100-pound trained bear.

At Clemson, William played nose guard.

William was a natural athlete. He started playing Pee Wee football. Pee Wee football charged a fee. The Perry family didn't have extra money. William didn't even get an allowance. He mowed the school grounds. That money paid for Pee Wee football.

By eighth grade, William weighed about 240 pounds. In high school William played basketball. He averaged 18 points a game. Many colleges wanted William. They thought he was a good athlete. Auburn, Michigan, Michigan State, Ohio State, Tennessee, and UCLA wanted him.

William and Sherry were married when he was still in college.

But William wanted to stay near his family. He wanted to be near his girlfriend, Sherry. He chose a college close to home. He decided to go to Clemson University. Then he would be able to go home on weekends. He could visit his family. He could see his girlfriend.

As a freshman, William weighed 285 pounds. He was tall, too. He was nicknamed "G.E." Why "G.E."? Because he looked as big as a refrigerator.

William played football. He helped Clemson's team. They had a perfect record. They won 11 games. They lost no games. They won their first national championship.

William "the Refrigerator" played football all four years at Clemson. His senior year, 1984, was his best. He returned a blocked punt for 35 yards. He recovered or caused 15 fumbles. He sacked the quarterback 25 times. That was a conference record. In his senior year, William weighed 335 pounds. He really was like a refrigerator.

Then William joined the Bears. At first he didn't play much. The fans still wondered about him. Could the Refrigerator play? Five games were played. Nobody knew much about William.

In his senior year, William was a finalist for the Lombardi college lineman-of-the-year award. Also nominated for the award were Tony DeGrate, University of Texas (far left) and Jack Del Rio, University of Southern California (center).

At first, William didn't play in very many games. But then he was sent in and he sacked the quarterback (left).

Then came the sixth game. The Bears were playing the San Francisco 49ers. They were the defending Super Bowl team. The 49ers had creamed the Bears the year before. It was a shutout. They won 23 to 0. The Bears remembered that.

William "the Refrigerator" was sent into the game. He was part of a special team. He played defense. He did well and the fans liked it.

William played with the offense too. Jim McMahon was the quarterback. He handed the football to William. William ran with the ball.

William and teammate Mike Singletary

Quarterback McMahon is ready to hand the ball to the Refrigerator.

He was a running back! The fans loved it. William "the Refrigerator" fever started. Now the fans knew what William could do. Other teams knew too. The Refrigerator was a threat. They would have to stop him.

The Bears had a Monday night game. It was on national television. They played the Green Bay Packers. William "the Refrigerator" played. He blocked for running back Walter Payton. His blocks helped Payton score touchdowns.

The Packers watched the Refrigerator. They had to stop him blocking for Payton. But quar-

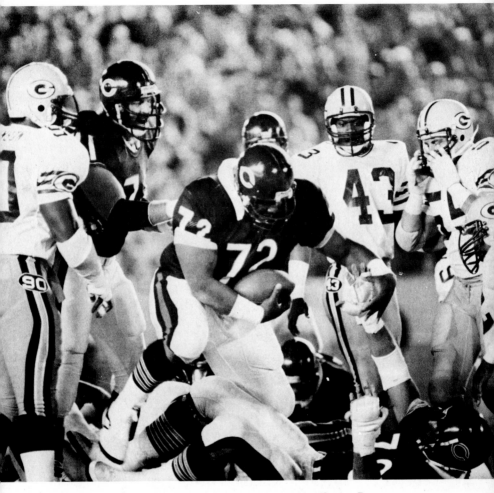

Above: The Refrigerator makes a touchdown against Green Bay.

Left: William and Walter Payton celebrate Payton's second touchdown.

terback McMahon fooled the Packers. He didn't have the Refrigerator block. He handed the ball to William. The Refrigerator ran through the Packers line. He scored a touchdown. It was his first touchdown as a pro.

The Bears won. Now the fans knew why Ditka picked William Perry. The Refrigerator was a national hero.

Two weeks later the Bears played Green Bay again. The Refrigerator was playing offense. So was Walter Payton. The Packers thought William would block for Payton. They thought he

Before Super Bowl XX, the Refrigerator practiced throwing the ball.

would carry the ball for a touchdown. But no, McMahon fooled them. He threw a pass. The Refrigerator caught it. It was a touchdown.

Now *everyone* knew who William "the Refrigerator" Perry was. He was on television. Fan clubs started throughout the country. Reporters interviewed William. He made commercials. Bear fans were glad William was on their team.

William "the Refrigerator" Perry is a big, gentle, happy man. He is married to his high school sweetheart, Sherry Broadwater. They have two daughters, Latavia and Norie. William likes to spend time with his wife and daughters.

William also likes to cook. He spends lots of time in the kitchen. But he isn't always eating. He can cook just about anything. He learned how to cook from his mother.

William appeared on David Letterman's talk show.

The Refrigerettes were formed to cheer for the Refrigerator.

When William goes home to Aiken, South Carolina, he plays basketball. He also likes to fish. Sherry's father and brothers taught him how to fish. He likes to go out all day. They fish on Lake Murray. They try to catch crappie or bass. William enjoys fishing, even if he doesn't catch anything.

What will William do when he retires from football? He wants to go back to South Carolina. He would like to work with children. He would like to help them have good lives.

William plays hard for the Bears. The Bears were the best team in 1985. They went all the way to the Super Bowl.

William cuts his birthday cake while his wife, Sherry, watches. Latavia samples the frosting.

Usually William "the Refrigerator" plays on the defense. He is a lineman. He is a good blocker. He has sacked the quarterback and recovered fumbles.

During the Super Bowl, William played with the defense. But a few times, when the Bears were near the goal line, they sent in William. Once, McMahon gave him the ball. He scored a touchdown.

After the Bears won the Super Bowl, William became even more popular. He made more commercials. He recorded a rap song and video with his teammate Walter Payton. He was a guest star on an episode of "The A-Team." He even wrestled in a "battle royal" with 25 other men in Wrestle-Mania, and nearly won.

William "the Refrigerator" would like to work with youngsters when he retires from football.

William continued to be very popular. A survey asked American teenagers to name their favorite sports hero. The athlete named most often was William Perry.

In the 1986 football season, William missed some games because of a knee injury. He also was heavier than the coaches had asked him to be. The Bears played well that season, but they didn't make it to the Super Bowl. They were beaten by the Washington Redskins in the playoffs.

William had weight problems the next year, too. He continued to play on both the offensive and defensive teams. By the end of the season he weighed over 360 pounds—more than he weighed in college. The coaches benched William.

William "the Refrigerator" Perry is a big, gentle, happy man.

William had more troubles the next year. His mother died during the winter of 1988. William was very close to his mother. He was very upset when she died.

At training camp, William weighed in at 377 pounds. This was the heaviest he had ever been as a Chicago Bear. He was still working hard to be a good football player, but he couldn't lose enough weight.

William decided he had to do something about his weight problem. He decided to enter a clinic for people with eating troubles. At the clinic, he could work to lose weight. Doctors could watch how much he ate. They could teach him not to overeat so often.

William spent a month at the clinic. His coaches and teammates were proud of him. They thought it took real courage for William to admit he had an eating problem.

William was eager to start playing football again. He worked hard at it. But bad luck struck again. In the third game of the season, William broke his arm. He was out for the rest of the season. He was very disappointed.

It takes a lot of work to be a football player. A player who doesn't work hard loses his place on the team. William works very hard to stay with the Bears. He is still one of their starting players.

William's youngest brother also plays pro football. Michael Dean Perry plays defense for the Cleveland Browns. He is the "baby" of the Perry family—6 feet tall and 280 pounds! On October 22, 1989, the Bears went to Cleveland to play the Browns. Several members of the Perry family flew up from South Carolina to watch the two brothers play.

William Perry doesn't make as many commercials as he used to. But that doesn't matter much. He still works very hard to be the best football player he can be. The fans know this. He is still one of their favorites. He is still the one and only "Refrigerator."

CHRONOLOGY

1962—William Perry is born on December 16 in Aiken, South Carolina.

1980—*Parade* magazine names William to the All-American Prep team for basketball.

1982—With William's help, Clemson wins their first National Championship with a record of 11 to 0.
— William is married to Sherry Broadwater. Latavia Shenique Perry is born.

1984—William is picked for the first-team All-American squad by Walter Camp, AP, and UPI.

1985—William plays in the Hula Bowl. The Chicago Bears select William as a defensive lineman.

1986—William scores a touchdown in Super Bowl XX. A second daughter, Norie, is born to Sherry and William.
— William is voted one of the four top Black Athletes of the Year for 1985.
— In an exhibition game in Wembley Stadium in London, England, William rushes for a touchdown against the Dallas Cowboys and receives a standing ovation.
— William plays both offense and defense for the Chicago Bears. The Bear defense sets a record for fewest points allowed in a 16-game NFL season (187, 11.7 per game), but lose in the playoffs to the Washington Redskins.

1987—American teenagers select William Perry as their favorite sports hero in a survey sponsored by the World Almanac. William records a rap song, "Togetherness," with his teammate Walter Payton.

1988—William's mother, Inez Perry, dies in Aiken, South Carolina.
— William enrolls in an eating disorder clinic to bring his weight down. In the third game of the season, he breaks his forearm and is sidelined for the season.

1989—William and his brother Michael Dean Perry play in their first professional game together.

ABOUT THE AUTHOR

Andre Roberts is a semi-pro football player in the Chicago Park District A.A.A.A. League. He enjoys traveling, reading, and writing poetry. He would like to someday be a teammate of pro William "the Refrigerator" Perry.

Other Lothrop, Lee & Shepard Books
by Jan Ormerod
Sunshine, Moonlight, Rhymes Around the Day,
101 Things to Do with a Baby, The Story of Chicken Licken

First U.S. Edition
1 2 3 4 5 6 7 8 9 10

Library of Congress Cataloging in Publication Data
Ormerod, Jan.   Bend and stretch.
Summary: A pregnant mother does her exercises together
with her small baby and the cat.
[1. Babies—Fiction.   2. Exercise—Fiction.
3. Mother and child—Fiction]   I. Title.
PZ7.O634Be   1987   [E]   87-2604
ISBN 0-688-07272-0

Bend and Stretch

Jan Ormerod

LOTHROP, LEE & SHEPARD BOOKS
NEW YORK

Breathe in and up.

Breathe out and down.

Left leg, right leg,
round and round.

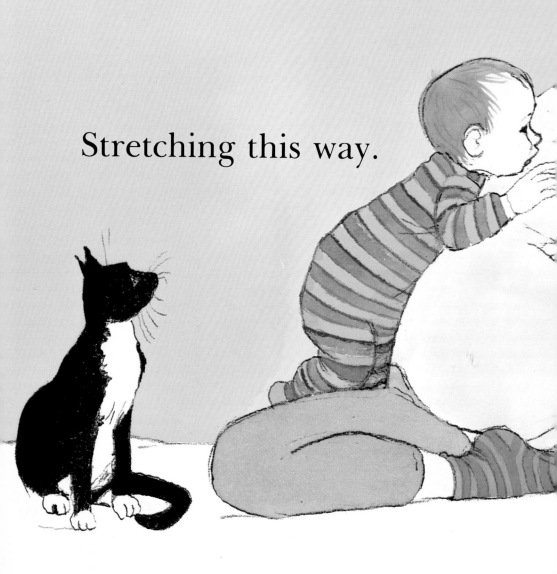

Stretching this way.

Stretching that way.

In, out,
   up, down,
      round and round.

Tickle, tickle, tickle.
Giggle, giggle, giggle.

Rest and relax.